MW00423811

To

_____

From

_____

Date

_____

Message

_____

_____

_____

_____

_____

BOOK *of* PRAYERS

The Power of
# PRAYER™
*to* ENRICH
YOUR
*Marriage*

## STORMIE OMARTIAN

HARVEST HOUSE PUBLISHERS
EUGENE, OREGON

Cover by Bryce Williamson

Cover photo © mikkipat, Boonyachoat / gettyimages

Back cover author photo © Michael Gomez Photography

Interior design by Chad Dougherty

For bulk, special sales, or ministry purchases, please call 1-800-547-8979. Email: Customerservice@hhpbooks.com

**The Power of Prayer™ to Enrich Your Marriage Book of Prayers**
Previously published as *The Power of Prayer™ to Change Your Marriage Book of Prayers,* now with extensive revisions and new material
Copyright © 2007, 2021 by Stormie Omartian
Published by Harvest House Publishers
Eugene, Oregon 97408
www.harvesthousepublishers.com

ISBN 978-0-7369-8243-6 (pbk.)
ISBN 978-0-7369-8244-3 (eBook)

**Printed in the United States of America**

20 21 22 23 24 25 26 27 28 29 / BP-CD / 10 9 8 7 6 5 4 3 2 1

# Introduction

Whether you want to *protect* your marriage from the things that can damage or destroy it, or you long to *mend* and *restore* your relationship where it has been broken or hurt, or you desire to bring peace and unity where there has been strife, the prayers in this book are for you. There is a way to pray about your marriage that can help you avoid certain common challenges, or enable you to mend a problem where it already exists. God has given *you* authority to pray for your husband or wife and invite the power of God to work in his or her life and in your lives together, as well as in your own life personally.

Under each of the 14 areas of prayer focus are four or five prayers. One or two prayers are for your marriage, and the rest are for yourself or your husband (wife) with regard to the area of prayer focus.

It is my hope for you that each and every prayer

in this book will be a starting point from which you will be inspired to continue on praying about the specifics of your own marriage. When you *pray powerfully* for your relationship, you will see God *work powerfully* in it. You will see *God do miracles* when you pray to the *God of miracles*, believing that He hears you and will answer. It happened in my life, and I am certain it can happen in yours. If you don't give up, your faith-filled prayers can strengthen your marriage so that it will last a lifetime.

*Stormie Omartian*

Whatever things you ask in prayer,
believing, you will receive.

MATTHEW 21:22

# 1

## *Pray to Keep Communication Open Between You*

*Lord,* I pray You would help my husband (wife) and me to be able to share our thoughts and feelings and refuse to be people who don't really talk to each other. Teach us to trust one another enough to talk about our deepest hopes, dreams, fears, and struggles. Teach us to spend time communicating with You every day so that our communication with each other will always be good. Enable us to openly express love for one another each day, refusing to speak words that tear down, but only words that build up (Ephesians 4:29). Show us how to listen carefully so we recognize the signs that give us greater understanding of one another.

In Jesus' name I pray.

*Let the words of my mouth and the meditation
of my heart be acceptable in Your sight, O LORD,
my strength and my Redeemer.*

**PSALM 19:14**

*Prayer Notes*

## 2

## *Pray to Keep Communication Open Between You*

*Lord,* I invite You to change me in the ways I need to be changed. Reveal any times when I have not said the right words or communicated the right thoughts to my husband (wife), and I will confess it before You, for I know I fall far short of Your glory (Romans 3:23). Teach me how to communicate openly and honestly so I will speak excellent, right, and truthful words (Proverbs 8:6-9). I know I cannot live in Your presence if I don't speak the truth (Psalm 15:1-3). Give me the right words for every situation. I pray that Your love will be so strong in my heart and mind that it comes out in everything I say.

In Jesus' name I pray.

*Though I speak with the tongues*
*of men and of angels, but have not love,*
*I have become sounding brass or a clanging cymbal.*

**1 CORINTHIANS 13:1**

*Prayer Notes*

_____

_____

_____

_____

_____

_____

_____

_____

_____

_____

# *Pray to Keep Communication Open Between You*

*Lord,* You are greater than anything I face and stronger than all that opposes me and our marriage. I pray that Your love will be so strong in my heart and mind that it comes out in everything I say. Help me to remember to show appreciation to my husband (wife) for the good things he (she) does. Open my eyes if I am not seeing all of them. Give me ears to really hear what my husband (wife) is saying so that I can bear some of his (her) burdens by simply listening. Make me quick to hear and slow to speak (James 1:19). Give me the wisdom to have a good sense of timing.

In Jesus' name I pray.

*We all stumble in many things.*
*If anyone does not stumble in word, he is a perfect*
*man, able also to bridle the whole body.*

**JAMES 3:2**

## Prayer Notes

## 4

## *Pray to Keep Communication Open Between You*

*Lord,* I thank You for my husband (wife) and pray that You would open his (her) heart to all that You have for him (her) and for our marriage together. Help him (her) to know You better, to understand Your ways, and to see things from Your perspective. Show him (her) how to view the two of us the way You do. Make changes in him (her) that need to be made so that nothing will hinder him (her) from fulfilling the purpose and destiny You have for his (her) life and our lives together. Show us how to find things we enjoy doing together so that we will always grow closer and never apart.

In Jesus' name I pray.

*Husbands ought to love their own wives as their own
bodies; he who loves his wife loves himself...and let
the wife see that she respects her husband.*

**EPHESIANS 5:28,33**

*Prayer Notes*

# *Pray to Keep Communication Open Between You*

*Lord*, help my husband (wife) to be honest about everything. Convict his (her) heart about any times he (she) has not been. Break down any belief in him (her) that deceit is acceptable. Strengthen him (her) to resist the father of all lies (John 8:44). May he (she) refuse to be snared by his (her) own words (Proverbs 6:2). Halt any division between us, and cause us to be of the same mind and have the same good judgment. Where he (she) has had trouble communicating well, enable him (her) to do so now. Thank You that You are our rock and our Redeemer, and You can redeem all things (Psalm 78:35).

In Jesus' name I pray.

*I plead with you...that there be no divisions among you,*
*but that you be perfectly joined together*
*in the same mind and in the same judgment.*

**1 CORINTHIANS 1:10**

## Prayer Notes

# *Pray to Keep Anger from Hurting Your Relationship*

*Lord,* help me and my husband (wife) to be "slaves of righteousness" so we will always do the right thing and never allow anger to control our lives in any way (Romans 6:19). Keep us from ever using anger as a weapon to hurt one another so that it drives a wedge between us. Fill our hearts full of Your love and peace so there is no room for anger, rudeness, or any kind of abuse. Teach us to pray about everything and make all of our needs known to You, knowing that when we do You have promised in Your Word to give us Your peace (see Philippians 4:6-7).

In Jesus' name I pray.

*Be angry, and do not sin.*
*Meditate within your heart*
*on your bed, and be still.*

**PSALM 4:4**

*Prayer Notes*

# 7

## *Pray to Keep Anger from Hurting Your Relationship*

*Lord,* help me to dwell on the good and the positive in my life and in my husband (wife). It is You who "looks deep inside people and searches through their thoughts" (Proverbs 20:27 NCV). Search the inner depths of my heart and expose anything that is not of You so I can be set free of it. Where I have directed anger toward my husband (wife) or held anger inside of me, I confess that as sin and ask You to forgive me and take all anger away. Heal any wounds I have inflicted in him (her) with my words. Help me to speak good words to my husband (wife), for I know that pleases You (Proverbs 15:23).

In Jesus' name I pray.

*Let every man be swift to hear,*
*slow to speak, slow to wrath; for the wrath of man*
*does not produce the righteousness of God.*

**JAMES 1:19-20**

*Prayer Notes*

# Pray to Keep Anger from Hurting Your Relationship

*Thank You,* Lord, that You will redeem my soul in peace from the battle that is against me (Psalm 55:18). I believe that You, the God of peace, "will crush Satan" under my feet shortly (Romans 16:20). Help me to live righteously because I know there is a connection between obedience to Your ways and peace (Psalm 85:10). Help me to "depart from evil and do good; seek peace and pursue it" (Psalm 34:14). Thank You that You will take away all anger in me, and any rudeness or abusive behavior I have exhibited at any time toward my husband (wife) or children. Keep me in perfect peace, because my mind is fixed on You (Isaiah 26:3).

In Jesus' name I pray.

*Above all things have fervent love for one another,*
*for "love will cover a multitude of sins."*

**1 PETER 4:8**

## Prayer Notes

_____

_____

_____

_____

_____

_____

_____

_____

_____

_____

# Pray to Keep Anger from Hurting Your Relationship

*Lord,* strengthen my husband (wife) to be able to control his (her) mind and emotions and help him (her) to remember that "we do not wrestle against flesh and blood, but against principalities, against powers," and the rulers of darkness and wickedness (Ephesians 6:12). Teach him (her) to be slow to anger the way You are (James 1:19). Direct his (her) heart "into the love of God and into the patience of Christ" (2 Thessalonians 3:5). Help him (her) to flee anger and pursue righteousness, godliness, faith, love, patience, and gentleness (1 Timothy 6:11). Help me to "lie down in peace, and sleep; for You alone, O LORD, make me dwell in safety" (Psalm 4:8).

In Jesus' name I pray.

*Cease from anger, and forsake wrath;*
*do not fret—it only causes harm.*

**PSALM 37:8**

*Prayer Notes*

_____

_____

_____

_____

_____

_____

_____

_____

_____

_____

_____

# Pray to Keep Forgiveness Flowing Freely

*Lord,* I pray You would help my husband (wife) and me to always be completely forgiving of one another. Help us to be humble enough to ask for forgiveness of each other when we need to. And give us a heart to forgive freely—whether the other asks for it or not. Help us both to "grow in the grace and knowledge of our Lord and Savior Jesus Christ" (2 Peter 3:18), so that we will become forgiving like You are. Help us to quickly forgive one another so that we will be forgiven by You, Lord (Luke 6:37). Teach us to love one another the way You love us and to always be merciful to each other.

In Jesus' name I pray.

*Whenever you stand praying, if you have anything
against anyone, forgive him that your Father in
heaven may also forgive you your trespasses.*

**MARK 11:25**

## Prayer Notes

# Pray to Keep Forgiveness Flowing Freely

*Lord,* thank You that we will have Your goodness and mercy following us all the days of our lives as described in Your Word (Psalm 23:6). Thank You that when we love each other the way You want us to, You will bless us and show us Your favor by surrounding us like a protective shield (Psalm 5:12). Lord, I know Your Word says that "if we say that we have no sin, we deceive ourselves, and the truth is not in us" (1 John 1:8). Help us to live in truth and be undeceived about our own errors. Enable us to be quick to confess our unforgiveness to You and to one another.

In Jesus' name I pray.

*Be submissive to one another,*
*and be clothed with humility, for "God resists the*
*proud, but gives grace to the humble."*

**1 PETER 5:5**

## Prayer Notes

# *Pray to Keep Forgiveness Flowing Freely*

*Lord,* thank You that "I can do *all* things through Christ who strengthens me" (Philippians 4:13), and therefore I have the strength to forgive my husband (wife) for anything that has hurt or disappointed me. Thank You that You are the God of forgiveness, mercy, and grace. Thank You that You have released me from any stronghold of unforgiveness. Take away all feelings in me that cause me to think I need to pay back hurt for hurt. Help me to "strive to have a conscience without offense" toward my husband (wife) (Acts 24:16). Where I need to be forgiven, help me to apologize and receive forgiveness from my husband (wife).

In Jesus' name I pray.

*Confess your trespasses to one another, and pray for one another, that you may be healed. The effective, fervent prayer of a righteous man avails much.*

**JAMES 5:16**

## Prayer Notes

# *Pray to Keep Forgiveness Flowing Freely*

*Lord,* I lift my husband (wife) to You in prayer and ask You to help him (her) let go of any unforgiveness that he (she) harbors. Help him (her) to forgive me for anything I have done—or not done—that was displeasing to him (her). I pray that You, "the God of patience and comfort," will grant to my husband (wife) the ability to be "like-minded" toward me so that we together may glorify You with a single-minded voice of unity (Romans 15:5-6). Give him (her) a heart of mercy toward me so that he (she) can truly let go of anything I have said or done that has hurt him (her).

In Jesus' name I pray.

*If there is any consolation in Christ, if any comfort of love, if any fellowship of the Spirit, if any affection and mercy, fulfill my joy by being like-minded, having the same love, being of one accord, of one mind.*

**PHILIPPIANS 2:1-2**

*Prayer Notes*

# Pray to Keep
## Negative Emotions from
### Affecting Your Lives

*Lord,* I thank You that You show us the paths of life and "in Your presence is fullness of joy; at Your right hand are pleasures forevermore" (Psalm 16:11). Thank You that when we delight ourselves in You, You will cause us "to ride on the high hills of the earth" (Isaiah 58:14). I pray that You will keep my husband (wife) and me from all paralyzing negative emotions. Help us to clearly see that we never have to live with any of them. Where we have allowed anything such as depression, anxiety, fear, rejection, or loneliness to influence our lives, deliver us out of all that and keep it far from us.

In Jesus' name I pray.

*You are my hiding place;*
*You shall preserve me from trouble;*
*You shall surround me*
*with songs of deliverance.*

**PSALM 32:7**

*Prayer Notes*

# *Pray to Keep Negative Emotions from Affecting Your Lives*

*Lord,* I pray that even though we may go through times when we are hard-pressed on every side, we will not be crushed, nor will we be in despair (2 Corinthians 4:8). We will rejoice in Your Word and the comfort of Your presence. We will not forget that You have the power to set us free. Your commandments are right and they make our hearts rejoice (Psalm 19:8). We were once in darkness, but now we are in Your light. Help us to always "walk as children of light" (Ephesians 5:8). I pray we will always look to You and put our hope and expectations in You (Psalm 62:5).

In Jesus' name I pray.

*He has delivered us from the power of darkness and
conveyed us into the kingdom of the Son of His love.*

**COLOSSIANS 1:13**

## Prayer Notes

---

## *Pray to Keep Negative Emotions from Affecting Your Lives*

*Lord,* I pray that You would "search me, O God, and know my heart; try me, and know my anxieties" (Psalm 139:23). Wherever I have allowed negative emotions to control me, deliver me forever from them. Show me things in my life that have been passed down in my family—attitudes, fears, prejudices, and even depression—and break these strongholds completely. Keep me from falling into bad habits of the mind and heart that are learned responses to life. I pray for healing and deliverance from any depression, anxiety, fear, rejection, loneliness, or any other negative emotion that would seek to find permanent residence in my heart.

In Jesus' name I pray.

*He shall cover you with His feathers,*
*and under His wings you shall take refuge;*
*His truth shall be your shield and buckler.*

**PSALM 91:4**

*Prayer Notes*

# Pray to Keep Negative Emotions from Affecting Your Lives

*Lord,* take away all sadness or despair. Heal every hurt in my heart. Give me a garment of praise at all times and take away the spirit of heaviness. Teach me Your Word so that Your glory will be revealed in me. Rebuild the places in me that have been damaged or ruined in the past. I pray that You would "send out Your light and Your truth! Let them lead me; let them bring me to Your holy hill and to Your tabernacle" (Psalm 43:3). May Your light in me completely evaporate any black clouds around me so that they cannot keep me from sensing Your presence in my life.

In Jesus' name I pray.

*He has sent Me to heal the brokenhearted…to give*
*them beauty for ashes, the oil of joy for mourning,*
*the garment of praise for the spirit of heaviness; that*
*they may be called trees of righteousness, the planting*
*of the LORD, that He may be glorified.*

**ISAIAH 61:1,3**

*Prayer Notes*

# Pray to Keep Negative Emotions from Affecting Your Lives

*Lord,* I lift my husband (wife) up to You and ask that You would set him (her) free from depression, anxiety, fear, rejection, loneliness, or any other negative emotions that grip him (her). Thank You for Your promise to bring out Your "people with joy" and Your "chosen ones with gladness" (Psalm 105:43). Thank You that because of You, Jesus, "darkness is passing away, and the true light is already shining" in his (her) life (1 John 2:8). Anoint him (her) with Your "oil of gladness" (Psalm 45:7). Restore to him (her) the joy of Your salvation, and uphold him (her) "by Your generous Spirit" (Psalm 51:12).

In Jesus' name I pray.

*You shall know the truth,*
*and the truth shall make you free.*

**JOHN 8:32**

*Prayer Notes*

# *Pray to Keep Your Marriage Strong While Raising Children*

*Lord,* I pray for your protection over our marriage and our children. Help us to learn how to pray for our children so that we never leave any aspect of their lives to chance. "Unless the LORD builds the house, they labor in vain who build it" (Psalm 127:1). I invite You to build and establish our house, our marriage, and our family. Help us to talk things through and be in complete unity about how to teach and discipline our children. Your Word says that You will reveal things we need to see when we reverence You (Psalm 25:14). Show us specifically what we need to see about ourselves and each child.

In Jesus' name I pray.

*He has strengthened the bars of your gates;*
*He has blessed your children within you.*

**PSALM 147:13**

*Prayer Notes*

_____

_____

_____

_____

_____

_____

_____

_____

_____

# Pray to Keep
# Your Marriage Strong
# While Raising Children

*Lord,* help me to be balanced in my parenting. Help me to not be obsessive about my children, but rather to relinquish control over their lives to You as I partner with You in raising them. Enable me to find the perfect balance between focusing too much on my children to the neglect of my husband (wife) and the other extreme of neglecting my children in any way. Give me Your wisdom, revelation, and discernment. Give me Your strength, patience, and love. Teach me how to truly intercede for my children when I pray. Show me how to pray so I can lay the burden of raising them at Your feet and have joy in the process.

In Jesus' name I pray.

*The mercy of the LORD is from everlasting to everlasting on those who fear Him, and His righteousness to children's children, to such as keep His covenant, and to those who remember His commandments to do them.*

**PSALM 103:17-18**

*Prayer Notes*

# *Pray to Keep Your Marriage Strong While Raising Children*

*Lord,* increase my faith to believe for all the things You put on my heart to pray about for my children. Teach me how to truly intercede for them without trying to impose my own will when I pray. I know that I don't have the ability to be the perfect parent, but You do. I release my children into Your hands and pray that You would protect and guide them. Help me not to live in fear about my children because of all the possible dangers, but to live in peace because I pray for each child and trust that You are in control of their lives.

In Jesus' name I pray.

*All your children shall be taught by the LORD,
and great shall be the peace of your children.*

**ISAIAH 54:13**

*Prayer Notes*

# *Pray to Keep*
# *Your Marriage Strong*
# *While Raising Children*

*Lord,* I pray for my husband (wife) to find the perfect balance between being focused solely on the children, and not spending enough time with them. Help him (her) to be willing to discuss with me about the raising and disciplining of each child so we can be in complete unity about everything. Help him (her) to see the need for us to spend time together alone so that we can stay strong and connected as a married couple. Lord, You have said in Your Word that whatever we ask we receive from You, because we keep Your commandments and do things that are pleasing in Your sight (1 John 3:22).

In Jesus' name I pray.

*The righteous man walks in his integrity;*
*his children are blessed after him.*

**PROVERBS 20:7**

*Prayer Notes*

---------------------------------------------

---------------------------------------------

---------------------------------------------

---------------------------------------------

---------------------------------------------

---------------------------------------------

---------------------------------------------

---------------------------------------------

---------------------------------------------

## 23

# *Pray to Keep*
# *Finances from Becoming*
# *Out of Control*

*Lord,* help my husband (wife) and me to remember that it is You who gives us the ability to produce wealth (Deuteronomy 8:18). And that the earth is Yours and everything in it belongs to You (Psalm 24:1). And that You, Lord, own every animal and creature and "the cattle on a thousand hills" (Psalm 50:10-11). All silver and gold and all things valuable belong to You (Haggai 2:8). Everything we have comes from You, so help us to be good stewards of the finances you give us. Help us to always be calm and wise in handling money so that we may prosper and not make hasty, rash, or impulsive decisions (Proverbs 21:5).

In Jesus' name I pray.

*The LORD will open to you His good treasure,
the heavens, to give the rain to your land in its
season, and to bless all the work of your hand.*

**DEUTERONOMY 28:12**

*Prayer Notes*

24

# Pray to Keep
## Finances from Becoming
## Out of Control

*Lord,* I know that having good health, a loving and supportive family, a solid marriage, great friends, good and satisfying work, and a sense of purpose in helping others is the richest life of all. Help us to always put our sights on those clear priorities. Lord, I pray that You would bless us with provision and help us to always be wise in the decisions we make regarding our spending. Help us to faithfully tithe and give offerings to You, and show us how you would have us give to others. Teach me and my husband (wife) to completely agree on our spending as well as our giving.

In Jesus' name I pray.

*The LORD your God will make you*
*abound in all the work of your hand.*

**DEUTERONOMY 30:9**

*Prayer Notes*

# Pray to Keep Finances from Becoming Out of Control

*Lord*, I pray that You will give me wisdom with money. Help me to be able to generate it and also spend it wisely. Teach me to give according to Your will and ways. Thank You that any charitable deed I do in secret, You will reward openly (Matthew 6:1-4). Show me when I am tempted to buy something I don't need and will regret later. Show me what is a waste of money and what is not. Help me to avoid certain places that are traps for me, where I will be tempted to spend foolishly. Help me not to be drawn toward things that will not add to our lives.

In Jesus' name I pray.

*Oh, taste and see that the LORD is good;*
*blessed is the man who trusts in Him!*

**PSALM 34:8**

*Prayer Notes*

# 26

# Pray to Keep
# Finances from Becoming
# Out of Control

*Lord,* reveal to me anything I need to see in myself that are bad habits with regard to spending. Help me to glorify You with the money I spend. I acknowledge You as the Lord who gives us the power to gain wealth, and I thank You that You give no burden with it (Deuteronomy 8:18). I know that I must not trust in uncertain riches but in You, for it is You "who gives us richly all things to enjoy" (1 Timothy 6:17). "Oh, how great is Your goodness, which You have laid up for those who fear You, which You have prepared for those who trust in You" (Psalm 31:19).

In Jesus' name I pray.

*He who is faithful in what is least*
*is faithful also in much.*

**LUKE 16:10**

*Prayer Notes*

_____

_____

_____

_____

_____

_____

_____

_____

# 27

# *Pray to Keep Finances from Becoming Out of Control*

*Lord,* I pray that You would give my husband (wife) wisdom about our finances. Help him (her) to trust You with all his (her) heart and not depend on his (her) own understanding (Proverbs 3:5). Help him (her) to not be wise in his (her) own eyes, but to fear You and stay far from evil (Proverbs 3:7). Give him (her) a good business sense and the ability to be responsible with money. Give him (her) the power to resist temptation when it comes to needless spending. Where he (she) has made mistakes with money, I pray that You would reveal Your truth to him (her) so it doesn't happen again.

In Jesus' name I pray.

*The God of heaven Himself will prosper us.*

**NEHEMIAH 2:20**

*Prayer Notes*

# 28

## *Pray to Keep Destructive Behavior from Establishing a Stronghold*

*Lord,* I pray that You would protect my husband (wife) and me from any kind of self-destructive behavior. Open our eyes to see if we have allowed habits into our lives that have the potential to harm us or others. Bring to light anything we need to see so that we will have nothing hidden from one another. If we ever open ourselves up to bad or destructive habits, help us to get free quickly. Give us the ability to cope with any frustration or anxiety we may be dealing with by taking all concerns to You and each other and not looking for relief from outside resources.

In Jesus' name I pray.

*Being confident of this very thing,*
*that He who has begun a good work in you*
*will complete it until the day of Jesus Christ.*

**PHILIPPIANS 1:6**

*Prayer Notes*

# 29

# *Pray to Keep Destructive Behavior from Establishing a Stronghold*

*Lord,* I pray You would reveal to me any habit I have embraced that is not Your will for my life. Break any spirit of rebellion in me that causes me to feel that I can do what I want, when I want, without regard for the consequences. Enable me to understand clearly how what I do affects my husband (wife) and family. Where You or other people have tried to warn me, give me ears to hear and receive the truth. Bring me to complete repentance before You for ever ignoring those warnings. Help me not to hold resentment toward anyone who tries to confront me on any problem, especially my husband (wife).

In Jesus' name I pray.

*All things are lawful for me, but all things*
*are not helpful. All things are lawful for me, but I*
*will not be brought under the power of any.*

**1 CORINTHIANS 6:12**

## *Prayer Notes*

_____

_____

_____

_____

_____

_____

_____

_____

_____

# 30

# Pray to Keep Destructive Behavior from Establishing a Stronghold

*Lord,* I cast my burden on You, knowing You will enable me to get free of anything that influences me in a bad way and to "stand fast therefore in the liberty by which" You have made me free. Keep me from being "entangled again with a yoke of bondage" (Galatians 5:1). I willingly present myself to You as a slave of righteousness (Romans 6:19). I know that I depend on the excellence of Your power to set me free (2 Corinthians 4:7). Thank You that I can do what I need to do because You enable me to do it (Philippians 4:13). My soul waits quietly for You to save me from myself (Psalm 62:1).

In Jesus' name I pray.

*My brethren, be strong in the Lord
and in the power of His might. Put on the
whole armor of God, that you may be able
to stand against the wiles of the devil.*

**EPHESIANS 6:10-11**

## Prayer Notes

# 31

# *Pray to Keep Destructive Behavior from Establishing a Stronghold*

*Lord,* keep my husband (wife) free from any destructive habits. Let there be no secrets. I pray that You, "the God of our Lord Jesus Christ, the Father of glory," will give to him (her) "the spirit of wisdom and revelation" in the knowledge of You, that the eyes of his (her) understanding would be enlightened, that he (she) would "know what is the hope of His calling, what are the riches of the glory of His inheritance" and "what is the exceeding greatness" of Your power toward him (her) who believes, according to the work of Your mighty power in his (her) life (Ephesians 1:17-19).

In Jesus' name I pray.

*Do not be conformed to this world,*
*but be transformed by the renewing of your mind,*
*that you may prove what is that good*
*and acceptable and perfect will of God.*

**ROMANS 12:2**

*Prayer Notes*

# 32

# Pray to Keep Destructive Behavior from Establishing a Stronghold

*Lord,* help my husband (wife) to understand his (her) worth in Your sight. Help him (her) to seek You as his (her) healer and deliverer, so he (she) can find total restoration in You. To my husband (wife) I say, "Sin shall not have dominion over you, for you are not under law but under grace" (Romans 6:14). I say that God has deliverance and healing for your life. I say, "The God of peace will crush Satan under your feet shortly" (Romans 16:20). Help him (her) to stand strong in all the freedom You have for him (her), Lord, so he (she) will reject any destructive behavior from controlling his (her) life.

In Jesus' name I pray.

*Stand fast therefore in the liberty*
*by which Christ has made us free,*
*and do not be entangled again with a yoke of bondage.*

**GALATIANS 5:1**

## *Prayer Notes*

# 33

# Pray to Keep Ungodly Attractions from Entering Your Mind

*Lord,* I pray You would protect my marriage from any kind of ungodly attractions in either of us. Keep those temptations so far from both of us that they never find a place in either of our minds or hearts. Pour Your wisdom and knowledge into us so that we are too wise and too smart to allow the enemy to sneak up on our blind side and throw temptation in our path. I pray You would not allow temptation to even come near us. Give us the ability to see danger in advance and the wisdom to not do anything stupid. Help us to "walk properly" (Romans 13:13).

In Jesus' name I pray.

*No temptation has overtaken you
except such as is common to man;
but God is faithful, who will not allow you to be tempted
beyond what you are able, but with the temptation
will also make a way of escape, that you may
be able to bear it.*

**1 CORINTHIANS 10:13**

## Prayer Notes

# 34

# *Pray to Keep Ungodly Attractions from Entering Your Mind*

*Lord,* help me to love You with all my heart, soul, mind, and strength, and help me to love my husband (wife) the same way (Mark 12:30). Thank You for my husband (wife) and for the marriage You have given us. I pray that You would search my heart and reveal any evil thoughts, attractions, or fantasies I harbor so I can be free of them completely (Psalm 139:23-24). I love Your laws, and I don't want to have conflict in my mind that brings me into captivity to sin. Thank You, Jesus, that I can find freedom from my flesh, which serves the law of sin, so that I can serve Your laws instead (Romans 7:22-25).

In Jesus' name I pray.

*When wisdom enters your heart,*
*and knowledge is pleasant to your soul,*
*discretion will preserve you; understanding will*
*keep you, to deliver you from the way of evil.*

**PROVERBS 2:10-12**

*Prayer Notes*

# 35

# *Pray to Keep Ungodly Attractions from Entering Your Mind*

*Lord,* I lift my eyes up to You in heaven (Psalm 123:1). I take comfort in the fact that You are my refuge that I can go to any time I am tempted to look at anything ungodly, or when I see in my mind that which does not please You (Psalm 141:8). Take away all that is in me that holds the door open for sinful and lustful thoughts. I rebuke the devourer, who would come to destroy me with temptation, and I say that I will serve only You, Lord. Thank You, Jesus, that You understand temptation and are well able to help me when I am tempted (Hebrews 2:18).

In Jesus' name I pray.

*Those who are of a perverse heart are an abomination to the LORD, but the blameless in their ways are His delight.*

**PROVERBS 11:20**

*Prayer Notes*

---

# 36

# Pray to Keep Ungodly Attractions from Entering Your Mind

*Lord,* I pray for my husband's (wife's) mind to be protected from all lies of the enemy and open to Your truth. Take all blinders completely off of him (her) so that he (she) can clearly see everything tempting him (her) to live outside of Your will as a set-up for his (her) demise. Help him (her) to fully understand what damage any degree of giving in to temptation to allow ungodly attractions does to our marriage. Open his (her) eyes to that danger and give him (her) strength to avoid situations and people that could draw him (her) into it. Turn his (her) eyes away from worthless things (Psalm 119:37-39).

In Jesus' name I pray.

*How can a young man cleanse his way?*
*By taking heed according to Your word.*
*With my whole heart I have sought you;*
*oh, let me not wander from Your commandments!*
*Your word I have hidden in my heart,*
*that I might not sin against You.*

**PSALM 119:9-11**

## Prayer Notes

# Pray to Keep
## *Love Alive and Hardness of Heart from Developing*

*Lord,* I thank You that You are "a sun and a shield" to us and because of Your grace and glory there is no good thing that You will withhold from us when we live Your way (Psalm 84:11). I pray that You would protect my marriage from any hard-heartedness that could develop between me and my husband (wife). Help us to not be stubborn or rebellious, refusing to set our hearts right before You (Psalm 78:8). Teach us both to "number our days"—to value the time you have given us together—so that we each may gain a heart of wisdom as you have promised in Your Word (Psalm 90:12).

In Jesus' name I pray.

*Keep your heart with all diligence,*
*for out of it spring the issues of life.*

**PROVERBS 4:23**

## Prayer Notes

_____
_____
_____
_____
_____
_____
_____
_____
_____
_____

# 38

# Pray to Keep Love Alive and Hardness of Heart from Developing

*Lord,* show me any hardness of heart in me toward my husband (wife). I want to confess it to You as sin and repent of it. Melt it like ice in the presence of the hot sun. Burn any solid, cold, heavy, frosty lump within me until it pours out like water before You. Take my heart of stone and give me a heart of love and compassion. Break up the fallow ground where nothing good can grow and life gets choked out. I confess to any sin of anger, resentment, unforgiveness, or criticism toward my husband (wife). Create in me a clean heart, and make my spirit right before You (Psalm 51:10).

In Jesus' name I pray.

*I will give you a new heart and put a new
spirit within you; I will take the heart of stone out of
your flesh and give you a heart of flesh.*

**EZEKIEL 36:26**

*Prayer Notes*

# 39

# *Pray to Keep Love Alive and Hardness of Heart from Developing*

*Lord,* give me the wisdom to do what's right so that I will walk in my house with a perfect heart (Psalm 101:2). Help me to seek You with my whole heart and hide Your Word in my soul and keep all of Your commandments (Psalm 119:11). Teach me to understand and keep Your law (Psalm 119:34). I want to stand strong in all I understand of You, knowing that You will strengthen my heart (Psalm 27:14). Give me a full heart of love for my husband (wife) every day. Thank You that You are a God of new beginnings. Help me to take steps that signify a new beginning in me today.

In Jesus' name I pray.

*Wait on the LORD; be of good courage,*
*and He shall strengthen your heart;*
*wait, I say, on the LORD!*

**PSALM 27:14**

## Prayer Notes

# 40

# Pray to Keep
## *Love Alive and Hardness of Heart from Developing*

*Lord,* I pray that You would give my husband (wife) a heart that longs to know You better so that his (her) heart will be soft toward both You and me. Where his (her) heart has already become hard, I pray that he (she) will turn to You and find Your presence waiting for him (her) (Jeremiah 29:13). Open his (her) heart to hear what You are speaking to him (her) (Acts 16:14). Help my husband (wife) to have a heart filled with truth and not open to the lies of the enemy. Keep him (her) from having any kind of a rebellious or stubborn spirit so that his (her) heart is always right before You (Psalm 81:12).

In Jesus' name I pray.

*A good man out of the good treasure*
*of his heart brings forth good things.*

**MATTHEW 12:35**

*Prayer Notes*

_____

_____

_____

_____

_____

_____

_____

_____

_____

# 41

# Pray to Keep
## *Your Priorities Clear and in Order*

*Lord,* I pray You would help my husband (wife) and me to always make You our top priority, and to make each other our priority under You. Make us to be vessels through which Your love flows. Show us how to establish right priorities in our marriage so we can be better for one another and better parents for our children. I pray that we will not do anything "through selfish ambition or conceit, but in lowliness of mind" may we esteem each other better than ourselves (Philippians 2:3). Help us to always find time for one another to be a help, support, encourager, uplifter, lover, companion, and sharer of good things.

In Jesus' name I pray.

*Humble yourselves under the mighty hand of God,*
*that He may exalt you in due time,*
*casting all your care upon Him,*
*for He cares for you.*

**1 PETER 5:6-7**

*Prayer Notes*

_____
_____
_____
_____
_____
_____
_____
_____
_____
_____

# 42

# *Pray to Keep Your Priorities Clear and in Order*

*Lord,* help us to choose each other and our children over the many seemingly important things that vie for our attention. I know that putting one another first does not mean neglecting our children in any way, but it is a position of our heart that says a good marriage is a gift we work to preserve *for* our children. Teach us to set aside time to be together alone. In our seasons of necessary busyness, help us to be in agreement as to how to handle those times successfully. Help us to always find our treasure in You above all else so we can give our children a solid home and family and our undying love.

In Jesus' name I pray.

*As for me and my house,*
*we will serve the LORD.*

**JOSHUA 24:15**

*Prayer Notes*

43

# *Pray to Keep
Your Priorities Clear
and in Order*

*Lord,* help me to always put You first in my life
and to put my husband (wife) next above everything else. Show me how to let him (her) clearly
know that this is what I am doing. I look to You to
teach me the way I should walk and what I should
do (Psalm 143:8). Reveal to me any place where my
priorities are off. Show me where I have put other
things, people, or activities before You or my husband (wife). If I have made my husband (wife) feel
as though he (she) is less than a top priority in my
life, help me to apologize to him (her) and make
amends for it.

In Jesus' name I pray.

*Seek first the kingdom of God and
His righteousness, and all these things
shall be added to you.*

**MATTHEW 6:33**

*Prayer Notes*

_____

_____

_____

_____

_____

_____

_____

_____

_____

_____

_____

44

*Pray to Keep
Your Priorities Clear
and in Order*

*Lord,* where my husband's (wife's) priorities are out of order, I pray You would help him (her) to realize he (she) needs to put You first, me second, and our children next before everything else. Help him (her) to see where he (she) must make necessary changes in the way he (she) spends time. Help him (her) to not feel so pressured by his (her) work that it overtakes his (her) life and our family suffers. Bless his (her) ability to work so that he (she) can accomplish more in less time. Enable him (her) to say no to the things which do not please You and are not to be high on his (her) priority list.

In Jesus' name I pray.

*Cause me to hear Your lovingkindness*
*in the morning, for in You do I trust;*
*cause me to know the way in way in which I should walk,*
*for I lift up my soul to You.*

**PSALM 143:8**

*Prayer Notes*

_____

_____

_____

_____

_____

_____

_____

_____

_____

45

# Pray to Keep
# Loss and Grief from
# Defining Your Future

*Lord,* I pray You would protect my husband
(wife) and me from suffering great loss and grief.
Keep us and our loved ones safe. Keep us from acci-
dents, plagues, or diseases. Keep us from losing our
abilities, good health, finances, and home. Thank
You, Lord, that if we do suffer loss, You will fill the
empty places in us that are there because of the loss
we have suffered. Even though things change in our
lives, You never change. You are never lost to us. You
can always be found. Where we have suffered loss,
help us to cast our burden of grief on You because
it's too heavy for us to bear ourselves.

In Jesus' name I pray.

*I will turn their mourning to joy, will comfort them,*
*and make them rejoice rather than sorrow.*

**JEREMIAH 31:13**

*Prayer Notes*

_____

_____

_____

_____

_____

_____

_____

_____

_____

_____

# 46

# Pray to Keep
## Loss and Grief from
## Defining Your Future

*Lord,* lead us through the process of loss when we feel we cannot live through the pain of it. Help us to grieve and not deny ourselves that healing process, and enable us to heal and get beyond it so we can have a good and meaningful life again. Lead us step-by-step each day so we can walk safely into the future You have for us. Thank You that with You nothing is impossible. Thank You that with You all things are possible. Thank You that You are acquainted with grief, and You have compassion on us when we grieve. Help us to always turn to You together as well as in our separate times with You.

In Jesus' name I pray.

*Blessed are the poor in spirit,*
*for theirs is the kingdom of heaven.*
*Blessed are those who mourn, for they shall be comforted.*
*Blessed are the meek, for they shall inherit the earth.*

**MATTHEW 5:3-5**

## *Prayer Notes*

_____

_____

_____

_____

_____

_____

_____

_____

_____

# 47

# *Pray to Keep Loss and Grief from Defining Your Future*

*Lord,* when I have experienced great loss and still find myself suffering grief because of it, I pray You would walk with me through this. I need Your comfort and healing power to work in me. Help me to not blame or resent my husband (wife) for any reason and put a terrible burden on him (her) that our marriage can't survive. I know that no one person can heal so great a loss, but You can. I worship You as my Healer, Comforter, and Restorer—my peace and the source of everything good in my life. I turn to You and ask You to lift the burden of this grief off me now.

In Jesus' name I pray.

*The righteous cry out, and the LORD hears,*
*and delivers them out of all their troubles.*
*The LORD is near to those who have a broken heart.*

**PSALM 34:17-18**

## *Prayer Notes*

_____

_____

_____

_____

_____

_____

_____

_____

_____

# 48

# Pray to Keep
# Loss and Grief from
# Defining Your Future

*Lord,* if my husband (wife) is suffering from a great loss and the grief that goes along with it, I pray he (she) would turn to You for comfort. Take all heaviness from his (her) shoulders, which are not built to carry it. You have promised that those who mourn will be comforted (Matthew 5:4). Your Word says, "The days of your mourning shall be ended" (Isaiah 60:20). Enable my husband (wife) to turn to You in his (her) sorrow so that he (she) will know the comfort of Your presence coming alongside of him (her) to walk him (her) through this to the other side of devastating grief and mourning.

In Jesus' name I pray.

*Your sun shall no longer go down,*
*nor shall your moon withdraw itself;*
*for the L*ORD *will be your everlasting light,*
*and the days of your mourning shall be ended.*

**ISAIAH 60:20**

*Prayer Notes*

# 49

# *Pray to Keep Working Toward Agreement and Unity*

*Lord,* I pray You would protect my marriage from the misunderstandings and disagreements that can happen when two people stop communicating. Help us to always be emotionally current with one another. Teach us to be kind when we could be stern, merciful when we could be judgmental, and forgiving when we could nurture an offense. Open our eyes whenever either of us is blind to what is going on inside the other. Show us where we are being preoccupied with other things and people more than with each other. Teach us to always be in agreement with each other and with You. Help us to be watchful about this.

In Jesus' name I pray.

*How good and how pleasant it is*
*for brethren to dwell together in unity!*

**PSALM 133:1**

*Prayer Notes*

# 50

# *Pray to Keep Working Toward Agreement and Unity*

*Lord,* Your Word says that You allow calamity to happen in our lives because of sin when we forsake You and worship other gods (Jeremiah 1:16). I pray that my husband (wife) and I will never depart from Your ways and become so wrapped up in other things that we begin to serve those things instead of You. Keep us on track and on the path You have for us so that calamity never comes near us. One of the greatest calamities would be to lose our marriage. I pray that it will never happen to us in any way. Give us revelation so that we can clearly see the truth (Proverbs 29:18).

In Jesus' name I pray.

*Two are better than one, because they have a good*
*reward for their labor. For if they fall,*
*one will lift up his companion.*
*But woe to him who is alone when he falls,*
*for he has no one to help him up.*

**ECCLESIASTES 4:9-10**

*Prayer Notes*

# 51

# *Pray to Keep Working Toward Agreement and Unity*

*Lord,* help me to always have a soft heart that is willing to talk things through with my husband (wife)—especially in areas where we disagree. I refuse to let myself become anxious about any sense of disunity I feel between my husband (wife) and me. Instead, I come to You with thanksgiving for who You are and all that You have done for us, and I let my requests be made known to You. Thank You that Your peace, which passes all understanding, will guard my heart and mind in Christ Jesus (Philippians 4:6-7). I will not let my heart be troubled, but I will trust in You instead (John 14:1).

In Jesus' name I pray.

*Teach me Your way, O L*ORD*; I will walk in Your truth;*
*unite my heart to fear Your name.*
*I will praise You, O Lord my God, with all my heart,*
*and I will glorify Your name forevermore.*

**PSALM 86:11-12**

*Prayer Notes*

52

# *Pray to Keep Working Toward Agreement and Unity*

*Lord,* where my husband (wife) and I have disagreements that are causing problems, I pray You would help him (her) to be willing to talk things through with me and seek You for what we are supposed to do. Teach us not to fight for our rights, but instead enable us to draw closer to You and closer to each other. Help us sense the love we have for each other and know that it is far stronger and more important than anything we disagree on. Just as no one can "separate us from the love of Christ," I pray that nothing will be able to separate us from our love for each other (Romans 8:35).

In Jesus' name I pray.

*Count it all joy when you fall into various trials,*
*knowing that the testing of your faith produces patience.*
*But let patience have its perfect work,*
*that you may be perfect and complete, lacking nothing.*

**JAMES 1:2-4**

*Prayer Notes*

_____

_____

_____

_____

_____

_____

_____

_____

_____

_____

# 53

# *Pray to Keep the "D" Word from Ever Becoming an Option*

*Lord,* I pray You would help my husband (wife) and me to always be able to rise above any thoughts of divorce as a solution to problems in our marriage. Keep our hearts so close to You and to each other that we never even speak the word "divorce" in regard to each other. Help us to always be affectionate to one another, "in honor giving preference to one another" (Romans 12:10). Show us where we are doing things that are breaking down our marriage instead of building it up. Teach us both to grow stronger in You so we treat each other in a way that pleases You. Enable us to stand strong together through every situation.

In Jesus' name I pray.

*Therefore what God has joined*
*together, let not man separate.*

**MATTHEW 19:6**

*Prayer Notes*

# 54

## *Pray to Keep the "D" Word from Ever Becoming an Option*

*Lord,* take away any ungodly attraction from our hearts and replace it with Your love. Show us what we can do to build each other up and be what we need to be for each other. Keep us from all pride, and give us repentant hearts before You if ever we are even tempted in our thoughts. Help us to be cleansed to become "a vessel for honor" for Your glory prepared for every good work (2 Timothy 2:20-22). Keep us far from anyone who would try to lead us into anything ungodly. Help us to always live in integrity before You and each other so that we will walk securely (Proverbs 10:9).

In Jesus' name I pray.

*If two lie down together, they will keep warm;*
*but how can one be warm alone?*

**ECCLESIASTES 4:11**

*Prayer Notes*

_____

_____

_____

_____

_____

_____

_____

_____

_____

_____

# 55

## Pray to Keep the "D" Word from Ever Becoming an Option

*Lord,* I pray I will not allow divorce to be a part of my thoughts at any time. If I have ever considered divorce in my mind or have seriously uttered that word to my husband (wife), family members, or friends in regard to my marriage, I confess that before You and ask You to forgive me. I know it displeases You and You hate divorce. I do not want to grieve Your Spirit, so I pray You would help me to never do that from this day forward. I smash down any dream I have entertained of being loved by someone else. I turn to You for solutions to any problems in my marriage.

In Jesus' name I pray.

*If any brother has a wife who does not believe,*
*and she is willing to live with him,*
*let him not divorce her. And a woman who*
*has a husband who does not believe, if he is willing*
*to live with her, let her not divorce him.*

**1 CORINTHIANS 7:12-13**

## Prayer Notes

# 56

# Pray to Keep the "D" Word from Ever Becoming an Option

*Lord,* I ask that You would keep any thoughts of divorce out of my husband's (wife's) mind and heart. If he (she) ever entertains those kinds of thoughts, I ask that You would open his (her) eyes to see how far away that is from Your best for his (her) life and our lives together. For any time he (she) has ever thought of the word "divorce" as a way out of our problems, I come before You on my husband's (wife's) behalf and ask for Your forgiveness. Forgive him (her) so that a spirit of divorce cannot find a home in his (her) heart. Let there be no divorce in our future.

In Jesus' name I pray.

*A man shall leave his father and*
*mother and be joined to his wife,*
*and the two shall become one flesh.*

**EPHESIANS 5:31**

*Prayer Notes*

---

---

---

---

---

---

---

---

---

---

# 57

## Pray to Keep
## Hope and Faith in the
## God of Miracles

*Lord,* I commit my marriage to You. May it become all You want it to be. Even in times where we may experience hurt or misunderstanding, I believe You are well able to keep all I have committed to You (2 Timothy 1:12). I pray You would help my husband (wife) and me to never fall into hopelessness, especially with regard to our relationship. Help us to always put our hope in You, for You are our helper and protector (Psalm 33:20). May Your unfailing love and favor rest on us (Psalm 33:22). Enable us to inherit all You have for us because we continually have hope in our hearts (Psalm 37:9).

In Jesus' name I pray.

*Everyone who asks receives, and he who seeks finds, and to him who knocks it will be opened.*

**MATTHEW 7:8**

*Prayer Notes*

_____

_____

_____

_____

_____

_____

_____

_____

_____

_____

# 58

# *Pray to Keep Hope and Faith in the God of Miracles*

*Lord,* I pray we will always have patience to wait for You to work in our lives and our marriage. Teach us to not give up on each other, but rather to "let patience have its perfect work" in us so that we "may be perfect and complete, lacking nothing" (James 1:4). Help us to "lay aside every weight, and the sin which so easily ensnares us, and let us run with endurance the race that is set before us, looking unto Jesus, the author and finisher of our faith, who for the joy that was set before Him endured the cross" (Hebrews 12:1-2). Enable us to keep our eyes on You.

In Jesus' name I pray.

*Israel, put your hope in the LORD,*
*for with the LORD is unfailing love and with*
*him is full redemption.*

**PSALM 130:7** NIV

*Prayer Notes*

_____

_____

_____

_____

_____

_____

_____

_____

_____

_____

_____

# 59

# Pray to Keep
## Hope and Faith in the
## God of Miracles

*Lord,* I come before You and cast all my cares at Your feet, knowing that You care for me (1 Peter 5:7). I thank You that Your plans for me are for a good future filled with peace and hope (Jeremiah 29:11). Help me to remember that no matter what is happening in my life and in my marriage, You will never leave me or forsake me. I commit to trusting You at all times. I pour out my heart before You, knowing You are my God of refuge (Psalm 62:8). Teach me to become like a child—entirely dependent upon You, for I know that this is the safest place I can be.

In Jesus' name I pray.

*Those who wait on the L<small>ORD</small> shall
renew their strength; they shall mount up with
wings like eagles, they shall run and not be weary,
they shall walk and not faint.*

**ISAIAH 40:31**

*Prayer Notes*

# 60

# *Pray to Keep Hope and Faith in the God of Miracles*

*Lord,* I release my husband (wife) into Your hands. I pray that any hopelessness he (she) has felt about himself (herself) will be taken out of his (her) heart. Make him (her) all You created him (her) to be. Break down any strongholds in his (her) mind where hopelessness has been allowed to reign. Help him (her) to put his (her) hope in You and understand that it is not by our might or power, but by Your Spirit that our relationship can be transformed to become all it was made to be. Thank You that You are the God of hope, and You are "the same yesterday, today, and forever" (Hebrews 13:8).

In Jesus' name I pray.

*Being confident of this very thing,*
*that He who has begun a good work in you will*
*complete it until the day of Jesus Christ.*

**PHILLIPIANS 1:6**

*Prayer Notes*

_____

_____

_____

_____

_____

_____

_____

_____

_____

_____

_____

# Other Books by Stormie Omartian

**The Power of Prayer™ to Enrich Your Marriage**

Stormie Omartian encourages husbands or wives to pray to protect their relationship from 14 serious threats that can lead to unsatisfying marriages or even divorce. Biblical, prayerful insights addressing communication breakdown, struggles with finances, anger, infidelity, parenting struggles, and more, will lead couples to healing and restoration.

**The Power of a Praying® Wife**

Stormie shares how wives can develop a deeper relationship with their husbands by praying for them. With practical advice on praying for specific areas—including decision making, fears, spiritual strength, and sexuality—women will discover the fulfilling marriage God intended.

**The Power of a Praying® Husband**

Building on the success of *The Power of a Praying® Wife*, Stormie offers this guide to help husbands better understand their wives and pray more effectively for them. Each chapter provides biblical wisdom, insight, and powerful prayers, and the book features comments from well-known Christian men.

**The Power of a Praying® Parent**

This powerful book for parents offers 30 easy-to-read chapters that focus on specific areas of prayers for children. This personal, practical guide leads the way to enriched, strong prayer lives for both moms and dads.

**Just Enough Light for the Step I'm On**

New Christians and those experiencing life changes or difficult times will appreciate Stormie's honesty, candor, and advice based on experience and the Word of God in this collection of devotional readings perfect for the pressures of today's world.